Curious Questions & Answers about...
Our Planet

"What activity do you do for fun?"

Curious Questions & Answers about... Our Planet

"Do you prefer early mornings or late nights?"

"How good are you at recycling?"

"Who is your best friend?"

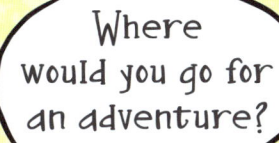

"Where would you go for an adventure?"

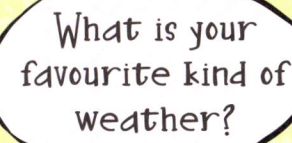

"What is your favourite kind of weather?"

Words by Camilla de la Bédoyère

Illustrations by Daniel Rieley

Miles Kelly

What is the Earth?

The Earth is a big, blue planet that travels through space. It is the planet we live on – in fact it is full of life!

Animals and plants live on the land and in the oceans too!

Is there life on other planets?

Not that we know of. There are living things on Earth because there is air, water, warmth and light.

It's night time where the Earth faces away from the Sun.

Why is it dark at night?

As the Earth travels around the Sun it spins, too. This means sunlight can only shine on one part of the Earth at a time.

Polar bear

Penguin

South Pole

Is Earth like a jigsaw?

Yes, because it's made of pieces that fit together! The pieces are called plates and they are made of rock. The thickest parts of the plates poke up above the sea to form dry land, where we live.

The plates float on hot rock

The plates are always moving very slowly and creating new land, seas and mountains

How do mountains grow?

Mountains are the tallest parts of the planet. Most of them grow when one plate moves and crashes into another plate. The rocks bend and fold, making mountains.

When plates move they can create earthquakes and volcanoes

How tall is the tallest mountain?

Mount Everest is the tallest mountain, and it is 8849 metres high. Everest is part of a group of mountains called the Himalayas.

Bar-headed geese are some of the highest-flying birds. We can soar over the Himalayas.

Mountain goat

Snow leopard

What lives on a mountain?

Nimble-footed snow leopards chase mountain goats across slippery slopes. Life is hard on a cold mountain because there is often snow all year round.

Mountains are millions of years old, but some of the rocks deep inside the Rocky Mountains could have been made more than a billion years ago!

CRASH!

Moving plates smash together

Hot rock

How are rainbows made?

Although we can't see it, sunlight is made up of all the colours of the rainbow. As a beam of sunlight passes through raindrops, it is split into seven colours. This creates an arc of red, orange, yellow, green, blue, indigo and violet bands in the sky.

Sunlight has all the colours of the rainbow in it

Light enters raindrops

Light splits into seven colours

Each colour of light is bent a different amount as it passes through the raindrop.

The colours bend inside

The colours leave the raindrops and make a rainbow in the sky

Why does thunder clap?

In a thunderstorm, the loud noise you hear is actually caused by lightning. The air becomes so hot from the heat of electrical lightning, it expands very quickly, causing the sharp clapping or rumbling sound we call thunder.

Why is snow white?

Snow is made of lots of tiny ice crystals. When these crystals become packed together as snow on the ground, they reflect all the colours of light by the same amount. When this happens, white light is made, which is why snow appears white to us.

Snowflakes are made of ice crystals, and every one is different!

Did you know?

The loudest **thunderclaps** can shake houses and shatter glass windows.

If **Mount Everest** were at the bottom of the deepest ocean, its tip wouldn't appear above the water's surface!

More people have been to the **Moon** than have been to the deepest part of the **sea**.

The Earth's **plates** move very slowly – sometimes as little 2 centimetres in one year.

Bees can see colours in **sunlight** that are invisible to us, but they can't see red!

When **moonlight** is bright enough you might see a rainbow. It's called a **moonbow**.

Because of the way the world spins, you would weigh less if you were at the **North Pole** or **South Pole**!

If you took off in an **aeroplane** at breakfast time on Monday, and flew all around the world, you could be home for lunch on Wednesday!

We have just one **Sun**, but in outer space there are at least 200 billion more suns!

The centre of the **Earth** is hotter than the surface of the Sun.

Huge piles of bat **poo** can collect in caves where bats sleep. The poo is so smelly that the gas it gives off can kill animals that want to move in.

Big lumps of burning rock can explode out of a **volcano**, flattening anything they land on.

Planet Earth is a giant **magnet**. Animals such as bar-headed geese use the Earth's magnetism to find their way when they go on long journeys.

The mega-hot conditions deep inside a volcano make water boil so hard that layers of solid **gold** can form!

The Andes are the longest chain of **mountains** in the world. They pass through seven countries!

When the world's deepest lake **freezes** the ice can be more than one metre deep. Cars can drive on it!

What is the water cycle?

The way that water moves around our planet is called the water cycle. Most of the world's water is salty.

Sun

Clouds start to form

Water vapour rises

Water is all around us, even when we can't see it. It's not just in the sea and rivers. It's also in the air and in the ground.

Salty water in the ocean warms up and turns into water vapour, a type of gas. This is called evaporation. The salt stays in the ocean.

People use fresh water to drink, cook, wash, grow their crops and give to their animals.

How many oceans are there?

There are five oceans, but they all join together to make one enormous World Ocean. Most of the Earth is covered with oceans and seas — about 70 percent!

At rocky shores, rock pools form when the tide goes out

What ocean animal is both big and small?

Coral is! It's a tiny animal that builds a rocky cup around itself, but billions of them together create a living rocky reef. A reef makes a great home for other animals too!

All kinds of animals live on a coral reef

Why is the sea salty?

Salt in the sea comes from rocks on the land. Rivers bring the salt from the land to the sea. Some salt also comes from rocks at the bottom of the sea.

> I'm a parrotfish. I nibble on reefs and make sandy poo. Golden beaches are covered in my coral poo!

What is the Equator?

The Equator is an imaginary line that cuts the Earth into two halves. Near the Equator, the weather is hot and sunny most of the time.

Arctic Circle

NORTH AMERICA

EUROPE

I am a jaguar, and I live in the tropical Amazon rainforest in South America.

The Sun shines strongly around the Equator, and there is daylight for 12 hours a day, every day.

Equator

SOUTH AMERICA

I am an emperor penguin and I live on frozen Antarctica with lots of other penguins, seals and birds. This is the coldest place on Earth!

Where does the Sun shine at midnight?

During the summer months in the far north of the world, the Sun doesn't set. In places such as Canada, Alaska, Russia, Greenland, Norway and Sweden the Sun can be seen in the sky at night. But in winter it is cold and dark all the time.

I'm a polar bear, and I live in the far north on the Arctic ice. I love eating seals!

I'm a tiger and I love the rain. I live in tropical forests of India, and I'm a very good swimmer.

AFRICA

ASIA

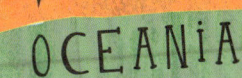

What is a rainy season?

Tropical places near the Equator are hot and humid. Strong winds called monsoons bring wet weather in summer. This is called the 'rainy season'.

ANTARCTICA

How many?

1 The number of years it takes the Earth to travel once around the Sun.

24 The number of hours in a day... because it's the number of hours it takes for the Earth to spin once.

365 The number of days in a year.

About **50** volcanoes erupt every year on Earth.

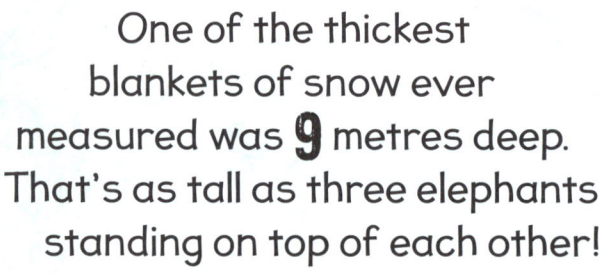

One of the thickest blankets of snow ever measured was **9** metres deep. That's as tall as three elephants standing on top of each other!

The sea freezes over near the North Pole in winter. The ice can be more than **3** metres deep in some places.

The deepest part of the World Ocean is called the Mariana Trench. It's about **10** km deep!

2 The number of summers enjoyed by Arctic terns every year. These white birds fly all the way from the Arctic to the Antarctic to get the best weather!

It takes about **1000** years for a drop of water in the World Ocean to flow once around the Earth.

In one year, **10,000** millimetres of rain can fall in a tropical rainforest, while less than one millimetre falls in the driest deserts.

1.3 million Earths could fit inside the Sun.

In the Antarctic, around the Earth's South Pole, temperatures can drop to **−50°C**, or even lower.

Earth is about **4.5 billion** years old.

In the last **50** years about one third of all Earth's rainforests have been cut down.

No one knows how many different types of animal there are on the planet, but it could be as many as **10 million**.

Are all deserts hot?

No, a desert can be hot or cold, but it's a dry place because it rarely rains. More rain falls in the hot and sandy Sahara Desert than in Antarctica, which is a frozen, windy desert that's covered in snow!

Pillar

Arch

Hoodoos

Why do desert rocks look so weird?

The wind picks up desert sand, and blasts it against the rock. Over time it carves out some amazing rock shapes such as hoodoos, pillars and arches.

Why do I need such big ears?

Those big ears help a fennec fox lose excess heat in the Sahara Desert. They're also good for listening out for burrowing bugs under the sand.

Why don't penguins get frostbite?

A penguin's body is suited to life at the Antarctic. Its thick feathers are like a waterproof blanket, and warm blood travels through the bird's feet so they don't freeze.

Penguins hold their eggs on their feet to keep them warm

Oasis

What's an oasis?

An oasis is a place where water can be found in a hot desert. It's one of the few places that plants can grow.

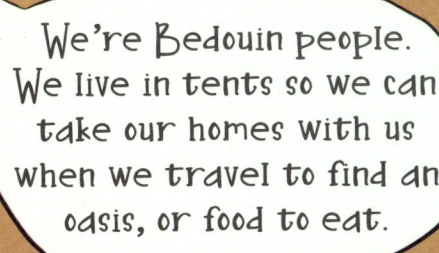

We're Bedouin people. We live in tents so we can take our homes with us when we travel to find an oasis, or food to eat.

Does it rain every day in a rainforest?

It can do! Rainforests are found in tropical areas around the Equator. The Amazon Rainforest is the largest rainforest in the world. It's in South America and is home to millions of animals and plants, from tiny ants to giant trees.

Monkeys and parrots feast on the tropical fruits

Why are plants important?

Animals need plants to survive because plants make oxygen. It's in the air, and we breathe it. Plants are also food for us and many other animals. When plants die they rot and turn into soil, which we use to grow more plants.

Rainforest plants have giant leaves and they grow flowers all year round.

The forest floor is home to fungi, frogs and billions of ants and other bugs

Would you rather?

Would you rather search for aliens in **space**, or travel to the bottom of the **sea** and discover freaky fish?

If you were frozen water, would you prefer to be a **snowflake** or an **icicle**?

Would you prefer to be as tall as a **mountain**, or as colourful as a **rainbow**?

What do we get from the Earth?

We get lots of things from the Earth! They are called natural resources. Animals and plants are used for food and clothing. We use metals and other minerals to make things. We can even use wind and water to give us power.

Plastics are strong and waterproof. They are often made from oil, which comes from the remains of tiny animals that once lived in the sea.

Glass is made from sand

"My bike is made of different materials that are found on Earth."

Rubber is a bendy, stretchy material that comes from rubber trees

Rocks are made of different materials called minerals. Metals such as gold and silver are minerals. Most sand is a mineral called quartz.

Metal

Fossil

Some fabrics are synthetic, which means they are made from oil or other chemicals

Pencils and paper are made of wood, which comes from trees

Rubber trees

Metal is hard, shiny and strong. It doesn't bend easily. Metal comes from rocks that were made in the Earth's crust.

Sheep fur is called wool and it is used to make fabric

Some fabrics are natural and they are made from plants or animal fur

Diamonds

Where do diamonds come from?

Diamonds are a type of mineral that forms deep below the Earth's crust. Diamond is the hardest natural material, but it can be cut to make sparkly precious crystals or 'stones'.

On 22nd April every year, people across the world take part in activities to help make our planet a greener place.

A compendium of questions

Will the Earth last forever?

Earth has been around for 4.5 billion years already but it's still very young for a planet, so there's no need to panic!

I'm still just a teenager planet!

Why don't we fall off the planet as it spins through space?

Thankfully, a special force called gravity keeps us on the Earth. It's a type of 'pull' force and the Earth, being heavier than us, pulls us towards its centre.

Can snakes live in the Antarctic?

There are no snakes in the Antarctic – snow and ice make it too cold. Snakes keep their bodies at the same temperature as the air around them, so they would freeze to death. They need warmth!

Why did my bike go rusty?

Bikes are made with a metal called iron. If iron gets wet (when it rains) the oxygen in the water joins with the iron to make a new material called iron oxide, or rust.

Why do planes fly above clouds, not below them?

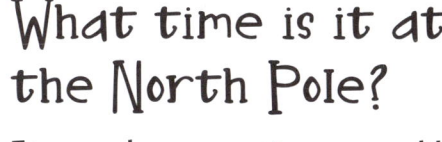

When planes fly, air pushes against them as they move forward. This is air resistance. Air is thinner above the clouds, so there's less resistance, making it easier to fly, and so use less fuel.

What time is it at the North Pole?

It can be any time you like! During the deep winter there is no day, and in the middle of summer there is no night, so 'time' doesn't mean the same thing at the Poles!

Always time for ice cream though!

Can cars run on chocolate instead of petrol?

Yes! Chocolate comes from cacao trees and it can be turned into a type of fuel called biofuel. Biofuels are cleaner than petrol, so that's good news (but a terrible waste of chocolate!).

What is a tsunami?

It's a giant wave that hits land and destroys everything in its path. At sea, the tsunami isn't too high, but as it nears land, the wave may be 30 metres high. It's caused by an earthquake under the seabed.